FOUNDATIONS FOR VICTORIOUS LIVING

Discipleship Basics for Spiritual Growth

DR. KERRY A SKIDMORE

Published by Ministry Resources Publishing

Unless otherwise indicated, Bible quotations are taken from the NIV Study Bible. Copyright 1985 by Zondervan Press.

PREFACE

Christians who have experienced the love, forgiveness, freedom, joy and strength that comes from receiving the Lord in their lives love to see others come into that relationship.

When others want to know Christ as Lord and Savior, we often leave them a little bewildered at that point. They may think, "I prayed the prayer of confession, I want Christ in my life, but what do I do now??"

This booklet seeks to give some guidance, structure and information to those who have just come into the Kingdom. If you are one of those, read it carefully, answer the questions, look up the Scriptures, and be ready to live a brand-new wonderful life you never dreamt possible.

You will have some problems, some temptations, and some difficulties will still come in your life, for this is earth, not heaven. There is a devil, and he continually comes against believers. But the good news is, that once you are a child of God, God will never forsake you, never leave you, and you will receive wisdom and strength for every circumstance of life.

CONTENTS

SALVATION

Congratulations! Receiving Christ into your life as Lord and Savior is the most important thing you will ever do. You must have done that or you probably wouldn't have much interest in this book! This book will give you guidelines and information that will help you not only be a Christian, but a strong, dynamic, confident child of God who will live a victorious life. These lessons are designed to help you become established and grounded in the Christian faith so that nothing will be able to turn you aside from your commitment to Christ.

New Christians are like newborn babies. They must learn to grow in their faith.

"Like newborn babes, long for the pure milk of the Word, that by it you may grow in respect to salvation." —I PETER 2:2

SALVATION

The moment you received Christ by Faith, many things happened, including the following:

1. Christ came into your life (Revelation 3:20)
2. Your sins were forgiven (I John 1:9)
3. You became a child of God (John 1:12
4. You received eternal life (John 3:16)
5. You began the great adventure for which you were created. (II Corinthians 5:17)

Nothing could be more wonderful than this! Let's look at what has happened to you. Here are some Scriptures for you to study:

"But God proves His love for us by the fact that Christ died for us while we were still sinners." —ROMANS 5:8

"For by grace you have been saved through faith; and that not of yourselves, it is the gift of God; not as a result of works, that no one should boast." —EPHESIANS 2:8-9

"For everyone who calls upon the name of the Lord will be saved." —ROMANS 10:13

"But to all who did accept Him (Christ) and trust in His name, He gave the right to become the children of God, who were born of God and not of natural blood nor of physical or human impulse." —JOHN 1:12-13

"For God so loved the world, that He gave His only begotten Son, that whoever believes in Him should not perish, but have eternal life." —JOHN 3:16

Read these verses and think about what these promises mean to you. Then complete the following sentence: "We are saved by faith or (b) works. Why did you choose the answer you did?

GOD'S <u>GRACE</u> HAS BEEN EXENDED TO US IN SALVATION. IT IS THE UNMERITED FAVOR OF GOD. We receive something we do not deserve not because of our goodness but because of God's.

COMPARE THE OLD LIFE WITH THE NEW LIFE:

The Old Life:	*The NEW Life:*
1. Fear of dying	1. Peace with God
2. Uncertainty	2. Assurance
3. Guilt	3. Clear conscience
4. Fear of God	4. Fellowship with God

ASSURANCE

Having assurance means being certain with freedom from doubt. One of Satan's tricks is to cause believers to doubt their salvation. Meditate on the following Scriptures to enable you to have victory over your doubts:

> *"These things I have written to you who believe in the Son of God, in order that you may know that you have eternal life."*
> —I JOHN 5:13

> *"My sheep hear my voice, and I know them, and they follow me; and I give eternal life to them and they shall never perish. No one shall snatch them out of my hand. My Father, who has given them to me is greater than all; and no one is able to snatch them out of the Father's hand."* —JOHN 10:27-29

The promise of God's Word, the Bible—not our feelings—is our authority. The Christian lives by faith (trust) in the trustworthiness of God himself and His Word.

FACT ⟶ **FAITH** ⟶ **FEELING**

We know we have been saved because we rely on the FACT of what the Bible says and our FAITH is in God and His word. FEELINGS are the result of our faith and obedience. Sometimes coming to Christ is a very emotional experience and people have lots of feelings. For other persons, there is little emotion involved. Feelings are not the barometer of whether we have been saved or not. Feelings change; we cannot depend upon them. God's word never changes!

Assurance doesn't come if we live in the past.

Assurance doesn't come if we doubt.

Assurance will not come if we depend on our feelings.

Assurance comes when we realize that eternal life begins the moment we trust Christ for our salvation.

A new birth is only the beginning; GROWTH is the goal!

G   Go to God in prayer daily (Matthew 6:9-13)

R   Read God's Word daily (Acts 7:11) begin with the Gospel of Mark

O   Obey God moment by moment (John 14:21)

W   Witness for Christ by your life and words (John 15:8)

T   Trust God for every detail of your life (I Peter 5:17)

H   Holy Spirit—allow Him to control and empower your life daily (Acts 1:8)

HOW TO BE FORGIVEN

"If we confess our sins, He is faithful and
righteous to forgive us our sins and to cleanse
us from all unrighteousness." —I JOHN 1:9

Although victory over sin is rightfully yours, there will be times when you miss God's perfect will. Whenever one fails or sins, Satan will immediately bring condemnation: "Now you really messed up. God hates you and won't forgive you." None of that is true. In His Word, God makes provision for his children who sin and come short of His glory. Forgiveness is being reconciled on the basis of obedience. We are children. Sometimes children mess up.

We receive God's full forgiveness as we confess our sins to Him. To confess a sin means to uncover it and call it exactly as God calls it. This honest confession must include a willingness to forsake the sin. God promises not only to forgive us but also to clean us and make us "good as new."

Any time the Holy Spirit shows you that some thought or action is hindering your relationship with God, be willing to confess that sin immediately and keep the channel between you and God and between you and others clear. You must always be as ready to forgive others as you want others to forgive you.

Think of yourself as a new person, a baby just beginning to grow. Say to yourself, "I am growing, I am learning, I am discovering, I am searching." As you do these things, you will grow and GROW and GROW.

BAPTISM AND THE LORD'S SUPPER

BAPTISM

After you have accepted Christ as your Savior and Lord, you need to be baptized. The Baptism of the spirit, or the new birth, is vitally related to water baptism, and yet the two are not identical. That there is a close connection between the two is attested by Jesus: "Truly, truly, I say to you, unless one is born of water and the Spirit, he cannot enter the kingdom of God. That which is born of the flesh is flesh, and that which is born of the Spirit is Spirit." —JOHN 3:5,6.

On the day of Pentecost, Peter exhorted the people to repent and be baptized. Paul proclaimed, "As many of you as were baptized into Christ have put on Christ." —GALATIANS 3:27

In the New Testament the gift of the Sprit does not always occur at the very same time as the sacrament of baptism. The disciples of Jesus had been baptized, but they did not receive the Spirit into their hearts until Pentecost. On the other hand, Paul's regeneration took place at the time of his baptism

(Acts 22:16) The Samaritans in Act 8 and the Ephesians in Acts 19 had both received baptism by water but had not yet received the Baptism in the Spirit.

The baptism in the Holy Spirit will be discussed in another lesson.

Water baptism is one of the two sacraments of the church and is the sign and seal of the new birth. There is only one baptism, and the Gift of the Spirit and baptism in water are its two sides. Water baptism is the outward sign; the Baptism in the Spirit is the inward reality. Baptism is an outward sign to those around us of something that has happened inside us, in our hearts and lives.

Consider the bride and groom at a wedding ceremony. Hopefully, when they meet at the altar before the pastor isn't the first time they've seen each other! They have grown to love each other and made a commitment to live their lives together. When they stand before the pastor and the witnesses, that is the time they declare to each other, to God, to those around them, and to the state of the love and commitment they have for one another. It is a fulfillment of their love relationship. So it is with baptism. We don't get baptized to become saved, but because we have been saved we will want to be baptized. It is an important witness and seal.

In baptism we are identifying with our Lord in several ways. First of all, we identify with Christ through his death. Paul writes in Romans 6:3-8:

> "Or do you not know that all of us who have been baptized into Christ Jesus have been baptized into His death? Therefore we have

been buried with Him through baptism into death, in order that as Christ was raised from the dead through the glory of the Father, so we too might walk in newness of life. For if we have become united with Him in the likeness of His death, certainly we shall be also in the likeness of His resurrection, knowing this, that our old self was crucified with Him, that our body of sin might be done away with, that we should no longer be slaves to sin; for he who has died is freed from sin. Now if we have died with Christ, we believe that we shall also live with Him."

Did you get the picture? Baptism by immersion gives us a wonderful picture of what salvation is all about. We go down into the water picturing our death, but then we are raised up to new life. Just as Christ died on the cross in order that He might experience the resurrection, so we too have resurrection life in Christ. We closely identify with Christ as baptism portrays our old life, our death to sin, and then our new life in Christ.

Another reason for baptism is that we are following the example of our Lord and we submit ourselves to this sacrament as an act of obedience.

When Jesus began His earthly ministry His first step was to be baptized. John the Baptist was baptizing many in the Jordan River, and He was amazed when Jesus came to be baptized as well. The Scripture records: "But John tried to prevent Him saying, 'I have need to be baptized by you, and do you come to me?' But Jesus answering said to him, 'Permit it at this time, for in this way it is fitting for us to fulfill all righteousness.'"

If Jesus felt the need for baptism, none of us should decide that we can do without it. It is an act of submission and obedience to present yourself for baptism.

In the New Testament, baptism was a public testimony of faith. It is also a means by which faith is strengthened and even fulfilled. We often give an opportunity for people to give a public witness about how God has been working in their lives at that time.

This brings us to the question of infant baptism. Since infants cannot have faith, it is it right for them to be baptized? The New Testament answer is that the promises given to the parents extend to the children (Acts 2:39) and our Lord expressly wished to receive the little children into His presence (Luke 18:16). Moreover, there is evidence that the practice of infant baptism goes back to the first Christians where whole households came to faith in Christ and were baptized (Acts 16:33; 18;8; I Cor 1:16). Certainly in these households there would have been children and infants.

Parents have a great responsibility to teach their children the things of God.

Infants and children that have been baptized need to have a time in their lives as they reach the age of accountability, when they will affirm for themselves their faith in the saving work of Jesus Christ. Many churches have a time of "Confirmation" when a child confirms for himself the promises made on his behalf by his parents. In the case of infant baptism, one is baptized toward faith rather than into faith.

Some churches and denominations don't agree with this, but feel it is best for parents to bring infants and children to the Lord to dedicate them and let them later learn about faith in Christ and be baptized.

The main thing here in both of these streams of thought is that parents should rear their children in the knowledge and things of God so they will have good understanding of what it means to be a follower of Christ by the time they have reached the age of accountability.

There are churches who offer three methods of baptism: immersion, pouring or sprinkling. There is some scriptural basis for this. Hebrews 10;22 says, "Draw near with a true heart in full assurance of faith, with our hearts sprinkled clean from an evil conscience and our bodies washed with pure water." The main ingredient for baptism is a sincere and contrite heart. Water is also needed, but how much water? While immersion is a wonderful medium for baptism and represents the full picture of being dead to sin and coming alive to Christ, many, because of health or other situations, cannot be immersed. Baptism shouldn't be denied to them for these reasons. If the heart is right and the sacrament is enacted in front of witnesses, there is no reason to believe this is in any way a lessor kind of baptism.

Baptism is a sign of God's wonderful grace poured out for us in Jesus Christ and sealed in our heats by the Holy Spirit. It is a sign that God elects us before we decide for him, that God's grace is the basis for our decision of faith. Yet baptism is more than a sign: it is a means by which the Holy Spirit comes to us and works upon and within us. Baptism plays a prominent role in our conversion and is not just a symbol of our conversion. This is because the

God of the Bible works in and through human instruments to accomplish his purposes among people.

QUESTIONS FOR REFLECTION:

1. Have you been baptized? At what age? How were you baptized?

2. If you have not been baptized, do you plan to be? How do you want to be baptized and why.

3. A sacrament is an outward, visible sign of an inward, invisible grace. Can you explain this in your own words?

THE LORD'S SUPPER

Baptism is one of the sacraments of the church and the Lord's Supper is another. Remember the definition of a sacrament: "An outward and visible sign of an inward and invisible reality or grace." When we receive the Lord's Supper we believe that something happens within us as we receive it. It is not just an external experience.

Do you remember when the Lord's Supper was established? It was the night when Jesus was betrayed into the hands of the sinners to be crucified. As he gathered his disciples for one last meal together, he instituted the Lord's Supper. This is the account:

"...the Lord Jesus in the night in which he was betrayed took bread and when he had given thanks he broke it and said, 'This is my Body, which is for you; do this in remembrance of me.' In the same way he took the cup also, after supper, saying, 'This cup is the new covenant in my blood; do this, as often as you drink it, in remembrance of me. For as often as you eat this bread and drink this cup, you proclaim the Lord's death until he comes." —I CORINTHIANS 11:23-26

The Lord's Supper that night was part of the Passover meal that Jesus was celebrating with his disciples. The Passover commemorates the time when the death angel passed over the homes of the Israelites while they ate the Passover Lamb and God then delivered them from the Egyptians. They celebrated that meal on an annual basis after that time. Jesus is the full representation of the Passover Lamb that delivers us and saves us from death. His death on the cross and giving his body and blood for us is a vital event to be remembered.

Some churches practice "closed" communion, meaning only members in good standing may participate. Most, however, follow "open" communion. That means that anyone can come and receive the sacrament regardless of whether they are a member of that church or not. We believe that Christ is the host, that it is his table, and we are not the ones to decide who can come and who cannot.

Some worry that they may take communion, or the Lord's Supper as it is also called, in an unworthy manner and won't take it for that reason. This should not be a concern. We don't come to this table as sinless people. Unless you are at church to belittle, blaspheme or make fun of the body and blood of the Lord, you are not taking it wrongly. All of us come in a less-than-perfect condition. Remember that at the last supper, Jesus offered the cup and the loaf to Judas as well as the other disciples, even though he knew Judas was about to betray him.

John Wesley believed that we receive grace into our lives as we participate in the Lord's Supper, and even that people can be saved through the taking of the elements. He said there was "converting" grace involved and he had witnessed unbelievers become believers as they partook of the loaf and the cup.

As we celebrate the Lord's Supper, we recognize three things. First of all, we look back and remember again Christ's gracious work for us on the cross of Calvary. It is with grateful hearts that we eat and drink, realizing that he gave his body and blood for us. Then we recognize our present condition. We are sons and daughters of God. We are blessed. We can receive grace and help for our lives as we experience anew the covenant that God has made with us. Remember that Jesus said that the drinking of the cup ratified the new covenant, the covenant that is written on our hearts instead of tablets of stone. Then, lastly, we think of the fact that Christ will come again. We "remember his death until he comes." Not only did he come once to be our Savior, he will come again in victory and power. We are to keep these three things in mind as we participate in the Lord's Supper.

Some churches call this event the Lord's Supper. Others call it communion, and others call it Eucharist. It is the same celebration.

It doesn't make any difference how the elements are administered. Sometimes people are invited to the altar to kneel and receive the bread and cup there. Other times, they may be asked to come by in a line and receive the elements while standing. In some churches, the trays are passed down the rows to people while they are seated. The method doesn't matter. It doesn't matter whether we use actual wine or grape juice. Some use wafers, others use a loaf of bread. The method isn't as important as what is happening in our hearts at the time.

Most churches allow children to participate. Jesus always extended the invitation "come" to little children along with the adults. It can be a means of teaching them, demonstrating our faith and a way of allowing God's blessings to rest on them. When children come home from church, it is helpful if parents answer their questions and explain to them what this sacrament is all about.

FOR YOUR REFLECTION:

1. Sometimes the sacrament is called communion, the Lord's Supper, or Eucharist (which means "joyful celebration"). Which name do you prefer and why?

2. What method has the most meaning for you?

3. What three things are we to remember in this sacrament?

THE HOLY SPIRIT AND HIS LORDSHIP

If you were to have someone come visit you, you might meet them at the front door. If they were someone you needed to talk to, you might ask them to come into the living room. If they were someone you felt very comfortable with, you might even ask them to come in around the kitchen table! That's where intimate friends and family usually congregate.

But consider this. What if you were to invite that person in because they were a very important person. Then you said to them, "Sit here while I go about my life. I'll come back and talk to you now and then. Glad to have you here." Then you went away to all your activities, etc. That person would be *in* your home but wouldn't have a very important place in your life and activities.

However, what if you were to say, "I'm so glad you're here. You are the most important person in all my life. I can't do anything without you. Not only do I want you to come in and feel at home, I'm going to turn the entire house over to you. From now on, you're in charge. I'll live my life in this house however you would like me to do it." That's an example of real lordship.

We often treat God in an offhand way. "Wow, thanks for being here, Jesus. I was pretty worried about what might happen if I were to die still holding on to these sins. Thanks for taking them away for me. It's good to get to know you. I'm fine now, thanks, so I'll just take it from here on my own. See you around."

That's not what happens when we are truly born again. When we give our sins to Jesus, our *life* comes with it. We aren't really able to live that life all by ourselves. We need power to live the Christian life and tell others about Jesus. That power has to come from an outside source—God. God, through the agency of the Holy Spirit, comes into our lives and empowers us to be what he has called us to be. Just as Jesus was physically with the disciples when he was on the earth, when he ascended into heaven he gave us the power to have his presence with us constantly. That gift he gave us is the third person of the trinity, the Holy Spirit.

The disciples had been with Jesus for three years. During that time they had learned much from him, seen his miracles, even been taught to do them themselves! Wouldn't they have been able to go out and begin telling others about Jesus after his resurrection and ascension? We might think so, but Jesus knew better. He said wait. Wait for the promise of the Holy Spirit to come before you go do my work.

"But you shall receive power when the
Holy Ghost is come upon you."

On the day of Pentecost, as they were all gathered in one room, in unity of Spirit, the Holy Ghost came upon them.

> *"And when the day of Pentecost had come, they were all together in one place. And suddenly there came from heaven a noise like a violent, rushing wind, and it filled the whole house where they were sitting. And there appeared to them tongues as of fire distributing themselves and they rested on each of them. And they were all filled with the Holy Spirit and began to speak with other tongues as the Spirit was giving them utterance." —ACTS 2:1-4*

When this happened, the people outside heard the noise and then they heard the disciples praising God in all the languages of the people that were there. Peter took the opportunity and began to tell them that this was the fulfillment of the prophecy of Joel. (Joel 2:28-32)

In the Old Testament times, the Holy Spirit was present in creation in Genesis 1. The Holy Spirit empowered prophets, priests and kings who were God's special messengers, but the Spirit was not upon the "common" people. The prophet Joel gave the wonderful prophecy about a time when this would change; a time when all of God's people would be empowered by the Holy Spirit. This was fulfilled on the Day of Pentecost, known as the Birthday of the Church.

Now, you can have the holy Spirit living and dwelling in you to the same extent that Peter, Paul, John or any of the prophets, priest or kings experienced.

Without the Holy Spirit, we can not be born again. Unless God draws us to himself by his Spirit, we can not experience his presence and love. But there is a greater dimension to be claimed. Just as in the first example about the visitor to our home, the Holy Spirit can be not only our Friend at salvation, but the Lord of our life.

Paul says to us: "Now we have received, not the spirit of the world, but the Spirit which is of God; that we might know the things that are freely given to us of God. Which things also we speak, not in the words which man's wisdom teaches, but which the Holy Ghost teaches." —I Corinthians 2:12,13

How can we receive the Holy Spirit? The same way we received Jesus into our hearts and lives. We must ask. The Holy Spirit is the *dunamo*, the "power" of God. He is powerful and dynamic, yet he is also very gentle and gracious. He will not come where he is not wanted.

Remember that the Holy Spirit is not an *influence*, but a person. He is grieved by our actions. He can be quenched by our lack of belief. He can be resisted when we do not think we need him.

Jesus told his disciples, "John baptized you with water, but I baptize you with the Holy Spirit and power."

We pray to Jesus and ask him to baptize us or fill us with the Holy Spirit. When we fervently want God to come into our lives and take control, he will do so. He often does this instantaneously. Sometimes, it is over a period of time as we keep before him and refuse to turn loose of God until he fills us.

But he will not grant this great blessing when it is only a passing request that we really have no great desire to receive.

How will we know that God has answered this prayer for us?
By the evidence of the Holy Spirit. He gives:

1. **Power over the world:**
   The world masters and enslaves people who don't have the Holy Spirit. To one man it offers money. To another it offers power. To another it is pleasure, and to another, self. Paul wrote, "The world is crucified unto me and I unto the world." Galatians 6:14. The world no longer held any temptation for Paul because his heart held something greater.

2. **Power over the flesh:**
   The body which God intended for good can be reduced to a state where the imprisoned soul wallows in lust and passions. God gave every great experience and desire, but he also gave the power to use these in correct and uplifting ways. Satan wants to reduce us to little more than animals, but God's desire for us is on a much higher level. When the Holy Spirit enters the heart and sanctifies the soul, he does not destroy these desires, but he purifies and regulates them.

3. **Power over the devil:**
   The indwelling presence of the Holy Spirit destroys all doubt as to the personality of the devil. He is detected and his malice is felt and known as never before. He comes as an angel of light to deceive, but the person filled with the Holy Spirit has discernment and wisdom concerning his presence and his intentions. WE have power to cast him out, to bind and loose as the need requires.

The Holy Spirit will fill us with a heavenly language that will enable us to communicate with God in a wonderful way. The prayer language will be used in our private times with the Lord and it is often used with interpretation of tongues in the church when God wants to speak to the church to encourage, exhort or give direction.

After we have invited the Holy Spirit to come into our lives, we will receive both the fruit of the Spirit and the gifts of the Spirit.

> *But the fruit of the Spirit is love, joy, peace, patience,*
> *kindness, goodness, faithfulness, gentleness, self-control:*
> *against such things there is no law.* —GALATIANS 5:22

When the Spirit comes to live in your heart, you will no longer have to work at being more loving, more patient, etc. The greater the extent that He lives in you, the greater the extent that the fruit of the Spirit will begin to be manifested in your life. You will discover, as time goes on, that the Spirit is shaping you into the image of Jesus Christ. That is His work in your life. When we hold back and don't submit ourselves to him, His work is delayed. When you don't resist, that work is accomplished more rapidly. People will begin to notice a change in us. It's not a change we can bring about ourselves; it is a spiritual work.

Along with the fruit of the Spirit are the gifts of the Spirit. These are found in I Corinthians 12, 13 and 14. These chapters tell about the gifts of the Spirit that is manifested in the lives of the believer and how those gifts are to be used in the Body of Christ. Each believer has at least one gift as their primary gift, and many will have more than one. There are times when God will use you in a gift because of the need of someone, but then that gift isn't needed or used again. The purpose of the gifts is the building up of the Body of Christ and meeting the needs of others.

The fruit of the Spirit and the gifts of the Spirit reside with the Holy Spirit. If we haven't received the Holy Spirit, we won't have these fruit and gifts. We are still saved, but we won't have the power and fulfillment of God's work in us apart from the infilling of the Holy Spirit. The gifts and the fruit are part of the purpose of the Holy Spirit's work in our lives.

One of the gifts of the Holy Spirit that is so vital and uplifting for the Christian is the gift of tongues, or heavenly language that has been mentioned. Through this "prayer language" we may speak to God without having to battle our human minds and the limitations of our language. We can have a direct channel to God for worship and fellowship. Often when we don't know exactly what to pray about in a certain situation, we can just pray in tongues, knowing that the Holy Spirit will pray through us perfectly in the will of God about the situation.

Through praying in tongues, we build up our spirits. It's a way we might say of "recharging our batteries." As we pray in our spirits, it's like feeding our spirits and making them strong. Then, when problems comes, we have a fresh infilling of God's power to reach out and pray, touch, heal, witness, etc.

One of the greatest things that the infilling of the Holy Spirit and speaking in tongues does for us is to tame our tongues. In the Book of James, he talks about how unruly the tongue is. It is one of the smallest of our bodily members, but has great power for destruction. Try as we may, we can't always keep it under control and say the things we know are right and uplifting. By yielding this member to the Lord, we turn over one of the last strongholds of Satan in our lives.

There are, in a way, two different kinds of Christians. There are "spiritual Christians" who have not only asked Jesus to come into their hearts, but have turned over the control of their lives to him. Then there are "carnal" Christians who still live according to their desires, their "rights," the hold their habits have on them, etc.

Many want Jesus to come into their lives, but they still live fully under their own power and direction. They have simply added "God" to the things they consider well and good and needful for the good life. To put God fully on the throne of your life and to put all other things under his full power and control is another manner. We often call him "Savior," but not many will call him "Lord."

Will you? Will you make him "Lord of your life?" If you won't you will never live a victorious life. You will always be straddling the fence, not wanting to let go of the reins of your life, not willing to turn over the control of your life to Him. You'll be on God's side one minute, and living according to the pleasures and standards of the world the next.

When you make Jesus "Lord" and ask the Holy Spirit to come in and take over the control of your life, you can begin to say:

"Jesus, how would you have me live my life?"
"What things do I need to change?"
"How will you have me earn a living?"
"How should I treat my family?"
"How should I deal with my finances?
"How can I serve you and others?"

Will you make Jesus "Lord?" If so, pray right now, if you haven't already done so, and ask him to come in, fill you with the Holy Spirit, and take over your life completely.

APPLICATION:

1. Have you made Jesus Lord as well as Savior?

2. If not, why not?

3. Search your heart carefully and see if there are any "secret sins" habits, or other things in your life you are still holding on to.

4. How would you explain to someone else the difference between a spiritual Christian and a carnal Christian?

5. Of what value is speaking in tongues?

6. Of the fruit mentioned in Galatians, which one are you most in need of? How will you know when this fruit is developed in your life?

7. After reading about the gifts in I Corinthians, what predominant gift do you feel you have?

PRAYER: COMMUNICATING WITH GOD

Many Christians grow FAST...
Others grow SLOW...
Some just DON'T GROW!

The Bible compares the new believer to a new baby, but then immediately commands that the baby "grow up!"

"...in all things grow up into him (Christ)..." —EPHESIANS 4:15

For any relationship to grow and become meaningful, there must be constant communication. Prayer, talking with God, is the only way we can communicate with Christ. When a person becomes a Christian he discovers the opportunities that prayer offers.

Prayer is not only asking what we want and need of God, but offering what he wishes of us. Even though some praying comes naturally to a new Christian, we still must learn the discipline of effective praying. In this lesson we will see how prayer is the way we build a meaningful and intimate relationship with Jesus Christ.

Study these passages on prayer. After each one, write down what you learned about prayer from the passage.

a) Luke 18:1-8 Parable of the Widow
b) Luke 18:9-12 Parable of the Pharisee
c) Luke 18:13-14 Parable of the Publican
d) Luke 11:5-13 Parable of the Friend at Midnight
e) Matthew 18:23-35 Parable of the Unmerciful Servant
f) John 17:1-26 Christ's prayer

Summarize some of your conclusions about prayer after reading these passages.

God has many ways of speaking to us. He speaks through the Scriptures, through preaching, testimonies of others, through the beauty of His creation, and the prompting of the Holy Spirit. Prayer is our natural response to God's communication with us. Responding to God in prayer after he speaks to you shows that you are paying attention. Prayer is how the power of God is unleashed. Personal battles are won in prayer. The cause of Christ is advanced as we intercede for others.

HOW SHOULD WE PRAY?

We pray through the name of Jesus. Jesus is the only way to the Father. Jesus said, "I am the way, and the truth, and the life; no one comes to the Father but through me." (John 14:6)

Jesus is the only mediator between us and God. Jesus promises to give what we ask for in his name. If we are abiding in Christ, we can petition the Father with all the authority of Christ. We must ask in his name on the basis of who he is, not in our own name and who we are. Look up John 14:1.

As we come to the time of prayer, we need to come with a clean heart. Sin hinders our prayers (See Psalm 66:18). We need to have a forgiving spirit toward others (See Mark 11:25) because unforgiveness hinders our prayers. We need to come in faith (Matthew 21:22). A believing heart is necessary for prayer to be answered.

Our faith grows through hearing the word of God (Romans 10:17). As we learn more of the attributes of God, we learn to trust him more. The more we trust him, the more we can experience the reality of his love, grace and power in prayer. We cannot create faith; it is only given from God as we rely on his Word and his faithfulness.

WHY SHOULD WE PRAY?

1. To glorify God John 14:13
2. To obey God's command I Thessalonians 5:17
3. To have fellowship with God Proverbs 1:8
4. To communicate with God Psalm 69:13
5. To follow our Lord's example: Matthew 14:23
6. To achieve results for the glory of God Matthew 21:22
7. To uphold the leaders of our nation I Timothy 2:2
8. To have our needs met
9. For the help and provision of others
10. To grow spiritually Luke 6:28

There are probably many more reasons to pray, with the first and foremost being to have a close relationship with God.

First of all, prayer changes us, then the things around us. Prayer is ordained by God so that his purposes are accomplished on earth. The Bible records that weather was changed, people were healed, some raised from the dead and others released from prison because of prayer. We can experience those things as well as we pray. God has not changed and his power and purposes are still the same.

As a Christian, you need to be involved in two kinds of praying: private and corporate. Although you must have a daily time of private prayer, God expects us to pray together in the body of Christ in unity and He will only answer some prayers in a corporate setting.

WHAT SHOULD BE INCLUDED IN OUR PRAYER TIME? THINK OF THE WORD "ACTS"

A ADORATION

Acknowledging God's character and attributes. Reflecting on God Himself. Praising God for who He is and what He does. It is important to take this time to glorify God and to get our thoughts off ourselves and our own situations. When we start with our thoughts on God's greatness, goodness and power, faith comes more easily. The Scriptures tell us "... God inhabits the praises of his people." (Psalm 22:3. The definition of "inhabits" means "lives in." God lives in our praises and comes on the scene when we begin to praise Him. Praise is the appropriate way to enter God's presence.

C CONFESSION

Agreeing with God about your spiritual need. Responding to His holiness. Admitting honestly and humbly where you have failed or sinned. Why is confession important? Read I John 1:9 and Psalm 32:5 for the answer.

T THANKSGIVING

Thanking God for what He has done and for what He is going to do. Being grateful for God's care and protection, and every good thing that comes into our lives. Why is thanksgiving important? Find the answer in Ephesians 5:20 and Psalm 110:4,5.

S SUPPLICATION

Appeal for God's help by intercession—praying for the needs of others and praying for your own personal needs. Look up Colossians 1:9-12, Colossians 4:2-4, Matthew 9:37-38 and Matthew 7:7-8 to find out why supplication is important.

Using this "ACTS"ad idea may help give some structure to your prayer time.

BE READY TO RECEIVE YOUR ANSWERS TO PRAYER

If you know you are abiding in Christ, that you are controlled by the Holy Spirit and praying according to the word and will of God, you can expect God to answer your prayers.

Whatever we vividly envision, ardently desire, sincerely believe and enthusiastically act upon, must inevitably come to pass.

1. Imagine what will exist when your prayer is answered
2. Ardently desire the actualization of that scene—ask God for it
3. Sincerely believe that God will enable you to accomplish all that he has commanded you to do
4. Enthusiastically act upon that for which God leads you to pray
5. Mobilize yourself and others to help fulfill the Great Commission

Take along some paper and pencils. God may give you insights that you want to record. Perhaps you'd like to write down your specific prayer requests so that you can cross them off when they are fulfilled, giving the glory to God when the answers come.

Once you have prayed for something, keep your faith up concerning that request. Don't pray for something and then say, "Well, I prayed but I doubt that God will answer!" You have just defeated your own prayer! Don't allow your mouth or your thoughts or the negative words of others to hinder your answers coming through. Sometimes answers take time. God may have to arrange all kinds of things and work in many people's hearts for some prayers to be answered. The main thing for you to do is HOLD STEADY. If you can already see it, you don't need faith. Faith is for the "between times" until the answer comes. Don't give up, and God won't.

Pray about anything and everything. Sometimes people feel they should save the big, desperate situations for God. If you pray about the small things, you won't have so many big desperate situations! Whatever is important to you is important to God. Nothing is too big or too small for God.

SOME HINDRANCES TO PRAYER

Some people realize quickly that when they commit themselves to prayer, they have a hard time getting away from the interruptions of life. Once we begin praying, the phone rings, the doorbell blasts, the children cry, etc. Satan does not want you to pray and he will do whatever it takes to keep you from it!

If the phone rings, let it ring. If it's important, the other party will call back. You don't really have to answer the doorbell. If you were talking to the President of the United States on the phone, would you put him on hold while you went to answer the door? I doubt it! You'd consider that connection too important to break. Well, you're talking to the King of Kings and Lord of Lords. Don't let smaller things interfere. If the baby cries, tend to him but go right back to your task.

What if you get drowsy? This certainly happens. Try walking while you pray. Pray aloud. This can help a great deal. Try different postures in prayer. Some people like to sit, some kneel, others like to lie prostrate on the floor or walk and pray aloud. Find whatever works best for you.

The main thing, the important thing, is to PERSEVERE. When Satan finds he can't get you off the track, he'll finally ease up on his opposition.

Prayer is your lifeline to God. Form the habit of starting each day with prayer, and then learn to pray throughout the day as the need arises.

"Until now you have asked for nothing in My name; ask, and you will receive, that your joy may be full." —JOHN 16:34

"Call to me and I will answer you and tell you great and unsearchable things you do not know" —JEREMIAH 33:3

CORPORATE PRAYER:

Not only should you have a regular, private time of prayer, you need to pray with other Christians. Corporate prayer during times of worship are important and you should enter into those wholeheartedly. You need also, however, to be part of an on-going prayer group where you can intercede on behalf of others and for the work of the Lord through the church.

A prayer group will also help safeguard you from getting off-track in your Christian life. As we hear from the Holy Spirit, we sometimes hear from other spirits as well! The discernment of other Christians is an important safeguard for us. Trust big decisions to your group and ask them to help you pray and discern God's leading.

Seek out such a group. If you don't have one, form one! The Bible tells us that "One can chase a thousand, but two can chase ten thousand!" The Word also says that if two or more are agreed in prayer, anything they ask shall be done. We have power in unity to bind and to loose. Don't neglect this powerful, needful form of prayer. You will really begin to grow in your prayer life once you have made the commitment to be part of a prayer group.

QUESTIONS FOR REFLECTION:

1. What is your best time of day to pray?

2. What things cause you to be reluctant to pray?

3. Is it possible to change God's mind in prayer? The word tells us that it is! God gives us great authority to ask for changes in people's lives and in the situations and circumstances of our world. Are you willing to step out in faith and give it a try?

4. It is IMPORTANT that you learn to pray aloud. If a little child doesn't begin to speak aloud as he grows, we get concerned. As baby Christians we too need to learn to speak aloud. Don't be afraid if you don't feel you know big theological words. God doesn't want to hear those from you. He just wants you to speak your heart to him in a simple, sincere way. He will always hear a prayer offered in this spirit. Pray aloud right now and ask God to help you commit to a life of prayer.

5. Practice the ACTS format of prayer as you establish your prayer routine.

THE WORD OF GOD

"All Scripture is inspired by God and profitable for teaching, for reproof, for correction, for training in righteousness; that the man of God may be adequate, equipped for every good work" —II TIMOTHY 3:16,17

"Your Word is a lamp to my feet, and a light for my path." —PSALM 119:105

"Great peace have they who love your law, and nothing can make them stumble." —PSALM 119: 165

"Be ye doers of the word and not hearers only, Deceiving your own selves" —JAMES 1:22

Traveling alone in unfamiliar territory without a map is an uncertain way to go. No GPS, no phone, no help at all. Being a Christian changes all that. Christ becomes the guide with the Bible as the Guidebook. Jesus taught that the Word of God is our spiritual food just like bread is our physical food. "It is written, Man shall not live on bread alone, but on every word that proceeds out of the mouth of God." (Matthew 4:4)

John Wesley was a man of one book. He used and studied many different sources and authors, but he took his authority and truth for living from one book alone. He wrote in the preface to his standard sermons:

"God himself has condescended to teach the way: For this very end he came from heaven. He hath written it down in a book. O give me that book! At any price, give me the book of God!"

God's word must be taken in daily portions. There is no such thing as "instant growth" by reading the Bible in one setting and ignoring it for days. God is committed to the *process* as well as the *product*. As a new Christian, you must begin a routine of daily Bible reading. This needs to become as much a part of your life as personal care and meal time.

Our purpose of living as Christians is to both know God and to make him known. The Bible is the key to knowing God because he has revealed himself to us in this book. Sometimes we wonder about God's will and whether we are praying according to his will. The more we come to know God's plan and purpose of salvation for the world and the more we witness His character through the pages of Scripture, the more we will understand who He is and what His will is. People who constantly fret about the will of God would do better to spend more time just ready his "Will!"

FOR PRODUTIVE BIBLE STUDY:

1.   PRAY to understand the Scripture. Prayer prepares the heart
2.   READ to receive truth. Reading broadens the vision
3.   APPLY what you read to experience growth. Application produces change
4.   MEMORIZE to retain knowledge.

The Word of God is the foundation of the Christ-directed life. It is from the Bible that you learn all the basics for the Christian life. As God speaks to you through the Scriptures you come to know him and understand his principles for life and ministry.

IN BIBLE STUDY, YOU NEED TO HEAR, READ, STUDY, MEMORIZE AND MEDITATE ON THE WORD. In this way you will get a full grasp of God's word.

MEDITATION is prayerful reflection with a view to understanding and application—giving prayerful thought to God's Word and your life, with the goal of conforming your life to his will.

When we meditate on the word, we ponder what we've read. We let it go over and over in our minds and hearts. We can do this while we are working, washing dishes, etc.

Two questions to ask:
1.   What is the meaning of the passage of Scripture you're reading?
2.   How should this affect your life?

This kind of mediation in God's Word can be done as you hear the Word preached, as you read the Bible in your devotional time, as you pray and reflect on what you are studying and as you go over some of the verses you've chosen to memorize.

As you read the Bible, take it at face value. Look at things in context. Realize that sometimes there are phrases like "as big as a lion" that don't literally mean that whatever was being discussed was the size of a lion! The key word "as" should give us a clue. If the Scripture said it was a lion, then take it for face value.

It will be important for you to obtain a copy of the Bible in one of the modern translations. Here is an explanation of some popular translations and how they fit into the conversion from the original language to our language today.

Literal	Dynamic Equivalent		Free
KJV, NASB	RSV	NIV, GNB, NAB, JB NEB	LB Passion

Literal. An attempt to translate by keeping as close as possible to the exact words and phrasing in the original language, yet still make sense in the receptor language. A literal translation will keep the historical distance intact at all points.

Free. An attempt to translate the *ideas* from one language to another, with less concern about using the exact words of the original. A free translation, sometimes called a paraphrase tries to eliminate as much of the historical distance as possible.

Dynamic Equivalent. An attempt to translate words, idioms, and grammatical constructions of the original language into precise equivalents in the receptor language. Such a translation keeps historical distance on all historical and most factual matters, but "updates" matters of language, grammar and style.

The best method for new Christians is to begin with a paraphrase like the Living Bible and then later turn to a dynamic equivalent such as the New American Standard. As you try different versions, you will find the one that best conveys to you the Word in words you can understand.

Someone has said that for many people, the Bible is like a string of pearls, without the string. We get bits and pieces of Scripture here and there, but fail to see the connective nature of the Word. We don't see God's over-all plan and purpose that begins in Genesis and follows through to the last words in Revelation.

For new Christians, a good plan of Bible study is to begin with the Gospel of John, then the book of Romans, and then proceed to the beginning of the Bible and start a plan of reading a portion of Scripture every day. Try to get into a Bible study where the overall plan of the Bible is discussed. These are usually called "survey" courses. These courses won't go into great detail of each chapter, but they will give you a good overview.

Look at how the Bible is organized. This will help you understand what kind of literature each book of the Bible represents.

THE OLD TESTAMENT:

Genesis, Exodus, Leviticus, Numbers and Deuteronomy
These five books are called the Pentateuch. They give account of creation, of God's calling of individuals and nations, and the establishment of the nation of Israel.

Joshua, Judges, Ruth, First and Second Samuel, First and Second Kings, First and Second Chronicles.
These books give history and the meaning of God's people coming into the land of Canaan, the appointment of kings, and God's dealing with them.

Ezra, Nehemiah, Esther
After the people went into exile and God returned them to the land.

Job, Psalms, Proverbs, Ecclesiastes, Song of Solomon
Poetical books tell us how to relate to God and each other.

Isaiah, Jeremiah, Lamentations, Ezekiel and Daniel
The major prophets who delivered God's message to the people.

Hosea, Joel, Amos, Obadiah, Jonah, Micah, Nahum, Habakkuk, Zephaniah, Haggai, Zechariah, Malachi.
Called the minor prophets, but they often had a major message.

THE NEW TESTAMENT

The Gospels: Matthew, Mark, Luke and John
The accounts of Jesus' life, his birth, ministry, death and resurrection.

Acts
The account of the early church.

Romans, First and Second Corinthians, Galatians, Ephesians, Philippians, Colossians, First and Second Thessalonians,
The writings of the Apostle Paul to the churches.

First and Second Timothy, Titus, Philemon
Called the prison epistles of Paul.

Hebrews, James
Direction and explanations of the Christian life.

First and Second Peter, First, Second and Third John, Jude
Writings of the other apostles.

Revelation
The vision given to John of the culmination of God's plan.

Even though others may not do so, take your Bible with you to Sunday School and worship services. As the Bible is being read, follow along in your own Bible. The scriptures may be projected on the screen, etc, but get in the habit of looking them up in your own Bible. You will get better acquainted with where the books are and how it reads in the Bible you are using.

Some may use the Bible app in their cell phones or other devices. This is fine to an extent, but you need to see the words on paper and be ready to underline and mark as certain passages or words speak to you. Don't be afraid to mark your Bible. Mark favorite passages, promises etc. you want to remember and you will be amazed at how much this will help you in being able to memorize and quickly locate certain passages.

You speak to God in prayer, He speaks to you through the pages of his word. Keep both ends of the conversation going! Many people have trouble praying because they don't know the Word. Some have trouble reading the Bible because they don't know the God of the Bible. Both of these disciplines, prayer and reading the Word, are important. As you study and as you pray, the Holy Spirit will come and enlighten your mind and heart as to the meaning of the Scriptures. No one who truly wants to understand God's purpose and plan will be denied. God will be faithful. He will guide you and lead you as you commit yourself to His Word. Don't come to the Bible to judge it: rather, let the Word judge you.

From Ecclesiastes 12:13: "Here is my final conclusion; fear God and obey his commandments, for this is the entire duty of man."

QUESTIONS FOR REFLECTION:

1. What translation will you be using for your Bible study?
2. What time of day works best for you to study?
3. Find an in-depth Bible study or survey class and get involved
4. Memorization is important to spiritual growth: Find a verse or promise and work on memorizing it.

THE CHURCH: YOUR NEW FAMILY

Now that you have become a Christian, it is only natural for you to want to be with fellow believers. The best way to discover new friends who love Jesus and are part of the family of God is to attend church. How exciting it is to find a whole new family. Every true Christian is your brother or sister. This new family is the church which the Bible calls the Body of Christ.

Question: What does the church mean to you? Take a moment to articulate your impression of the Body of Christ to this point.

A formal definition of the church is the one that John Wesley adopted: "The visible Church of Christ is a congregation of faithful people in which the pure Word of God is preached, and the sacraments duly administered according to Christ's ordinance, in all those things that of necessity are requisite to the same." That definition is a little stuffy, but basically it is saying the church is where the Word of God is preached and where the sacraments are administered to the faithful disciples of Christ.

John Wesley further affirmed that:

1. The Church is one: He continually affirmed his stand against division and schism.
2. The Church is Holy. The holiness of the church has a two-fold foundation; it is the church of the Holy Spirit and the true members of the church are holy.
3. The Church is Apostolic. The church should follow the pattern set by the Apostles in the book of Acts.
4. The Church is Universal. Wherever there are believers in Jesus Christ, regardless of race or place, there the Church exists.

The church is a community of believers and it is also a place of mission and outreach to those who have yet to know Christ as Savior and Lord.

1. Regular attendance at church is vital. Consider these reasons:
2. Jesus set the example. He regularly attended the synagogue—the church services of his day. As his followers we seek to please him. He said, "If you love me, keep my commandments." (John 14:15)
3. The Bible commands it: The new Testament Christians had guidelines by which they lived. They became very strong in the Lord and overcame great obstacles to be a powerful church that reached the world for Christ. Their pattern was "Not forsaking the assembling of ourselves together… and so much the more so, as we see the Day approaching." Hebrews 10:25. In other words, as you see prophecy being fulfilled and the time of Christ's coming drawing nearer, you need to be together with God's people more often.
4. You need fellowship with others. You gain strength by associating with people who are strong. Since you face sin and all kinds of evils daily,

you need to get together with people who know the Lord and who live upright lives. Their faith can inspire you to more faith. Their friendship will become valuable to you.

5. Worship God with others. Great blessings come from joining others in praising and singing to the Lord. "The Lord inhabits (lives in) the praises of His people" Psalm 2:3. As God's people come together in worship they become a powerful force in helping one another and in influencing the entire community. Praising God gives Him glory and when many come together in unity and one accord he receives even greater glory and honor. You can watch a football game at home by yourself, for instance, but there's a different atmosphere when you are at the stadium with others. In worship, there is much greater anointing when many believers gather together.

6. Your family needs the influence. Your family needs to see that other families and other people believe the same God you serve. This gives them courage to face unbelieving friends and stay true. Children need to receive the teaching and instruction of the church and parents need the church's direction and encouragement. Parents need to know how to rear their children in the ways of God. Children and young people need to know what God says about behavior and decisions that will impact their entire lives.

7. The preacher and teachers have something to say. You should go to church to be taught the Word of God and have your faith strengthened by the preaching of the Word. Pastors and teachers have dedicated themselves to helping you know God in greater measure. As you seek direction for your life and want to grow in the things of God, God can speak to you through the ministry of pastor or teacher.

8. Church attendance offers participation in the ordinances. Look up Romans 6:3 about baptism and I Corinthians 11:24-28 about the Lord's Supper. It is important that we receive the means of grace offered through the sacraments of the church. Remember that the sacraments are an outward sign of an inward grace. As we participate in the sacraments, we are reminded again just who we are in Christ and what he has done for us. The sacraments can be the means by which God leads us, speaks to us, cleanses us and guides us.

9. In the church we find our place of ministry. The gifts of the Holy Spirit as well as the baptism of the Holy Spirit were poured out upon the church, not just individuals. It is here we are anointed for ministry and given authority and direction in developing our gifts and ministries for Christ.

10. There is safety as we submit ourselves to one another. Sometimes in hearing the voice of the Holy Spirit, we may also hear other voices who are not so holy! Left to ourselves, we can get into error and create great problems for ourselves. As we pray, worship and study together in an atmosphere of mutual submissiveness, we can receive correction and help in discerning God's voice. We need to be open to the reproof and teaching of others and not be offended. We will, in turn, be called upon by God to help others. We are to be helped and to be helpful. When we isolate ourselves from the Body of Christ, we can grow dim in our love for Christ and easily fall prey to the deceitfulness of Satan.

11. Through the church we fulfill the Great Commission. Again it was to the church, not individuals, that Christ gave the Great Commission. "All authority has been given to me in heaven and on earth. Go therefore and make disciples of all the nations, baptizing them in the name of the Father and the Son and the Holy Spirit, teaching them to observe

all that I commanded you; and lo, I am with you always, even to the end of the age." Matthew 28:18-20. The church has the responsibility of evangelizing the world and it is through the agency of the church that the gospel is spread to people who have not yet heard or believed.

Think a moment: How did you come to Christ?
99 times out of 100, it was through some ministry or activity of the church.

The Scriptures have been preserved through the ages through the church; the doctrines of the church have been defined and continued. The Good News we know and believe today has been able to reach us because of the activity of the church.

God intends us to be part of the Body of Christ, the visible expression of Jesus Christ's life in the world. Just as when Jesus was here on earth, he preached and ministered and cared for people. Today the "Body of Christ" of whom Christ is the head, is still carrying out those functions. As people see the Body of Christ fulfilling its calling, they also see Jesus Christ.

The Bible tells us "Christ loved the church and gave his life for it." We must love the church, regardless of its imperfections, and give it the same devotion we would give Christ.

How do you find the "right" church? Visit several. Make sure they are teaching the pure word of God and that they believe in the present day ministry of the Holy Spirit. See if they have classes and seminars where you can learn and grow. If you have children, see that they have places and leaders who will teach and guide your children. Are they reaching out to others? Are there ministries in the church where you could get involved? Let the Holy Spirit lead you to the right church. You will know it when you have that "just right" feeling.

QUESTIONS FOR REFLECTION:

1. John Wesley said that experience, tradition, reason and scriptures are those influences that primarily shape our Christian lives. Which of these four first awakened you to your need for Christ?
2. After going through the reasons for attending church on a regular basis, what is your number one motivation for being in services each Sunday?
3. What do you do to prepare yourself for worship each Sunday?
4. For whom is worship primarily intended: God or man? Explain your answer.
5. Have you experienced being changed through worship?

We have been discussing the purpose and nature of the church. Now let's turn our attention to a very important part of the church: its worship services.

Worship is the response that a person makes when the Eternal God reveals himself. Worship is an expression of love and honor.

First there is always submission followed by:

- Exalting the Glory of God Revelation :4:11

- Confessing the awfulness of sin: Revelation 6:5

- Give the sacrifice of self: Romans 12:1

- Requesting answers to prayer

- Thanking the Lord for his benefits

- Serving the Lord in faithfulness

WORSHIP IS EXPRESSED:

- In various ways: singing, speaking, writing, thinking

- In various moods: joyfully, meditatively, reverently, expectantly

- In various intensities: shouting, praising, exalting, yielding

- In various manifestations: kneeling, sitting, clapping, standing

Consider the following:

1. The heart of worship is the celebration of God. The most appropriate way to approach God is worship through praise and thanksgiving.
2. Praise focuses on the attributes of God. Praise is the expression of acknowledgement, approval, admiration, and adoration to God for what he is and for who he is.

3. Thanksgiving focuses on the actions of God. Thanksgiving is an expression of appreciation to God for being the source of every good and perfect gift.

Worship is unique. While praise and thanksgiving are a part of it, they can be directed to man. Worship is reserved for God alone.

Prepare yourself for worship on Sundays by being a worshiper all through the week. As you pray and study the Bible, also include times of worship and praise. When you come to church with a heart spilling over with joy and gratitude, you can imagine that the services will be much richer for you and because of you.

Each believer should do their part to come prepared to fully enter God's presence. When we come with the weight of the world on our shoulders, we must battle through this heaviness to obtain joy and the spirit of praise, and be ready to receive from God.

FOR FURTHER REFLECTION:

1. Jesus told the woman at the well that God was seeking worshipers who would worship him in spirit and in truth. How would you define Jesus' statement?
2. In which situations have you found yourself to be the most spiritually strong and full of faith?

Make it a regular practice to worship with others each Sunday. You are making a statement to God about your commitment to him and you are letting others know what is important to you. Satan trembles when believers gather for worship each Sunday!

ENTER HIS GATES
WITH THANKSGIVING
AND HIS COURTS WITH PRAISE

HOLINESS IN HEART AND LIFE

A Stanford University psychologist recently set forth a theory called "Cognitive Dissonance." It refers to a person's awareness of the big gap between ideals and actions, between what one believes and what one does, between an individual's goals and deeds. We feel this dissonance very strongly when we begin to talk about "holiness."

First we are justified, then we are made holy. We don't want to get the order wrong. Many people try, by good works, to make themselves pleasing to God and this never works. We come to Christ as we are and are justified by faith alone. We trade our sins to Christ and he gives us his righteousness in return. "For He delivered us from the domain of darkness and transferred us to the kingdom of His beloved Son" Colossians 1:11.

The Jews tried to be right before God by obedience to the law. They needed to understand the idea of liberty. They needed to develop a relationship with Christ. They didn't understand that they were sons.

The Gentiles, on the other hand, had been used to a life of licentiousness. They needed to understand obedience. They needed not the law, but a standard of how to live. They needed to become slaves.

As Christians, we relate to God both as sons and as slaves.

> *"And because you are sons, God sent forth the Spirit of his Son into your hearts, crying out, 'Abba; Father'"* —GALATIANS 4:6

> *"I speak in human terms because of the weakness of your flesh. For just as you presented your members as slaves of uncleanness and of lawlessness leading to more lawlessness, so now present your members as slaves of righteousness for holiness."* —ROMANS 6:19

This produces obedience to God's will. It produces Christlikeness. We are to be made into the image and likeness of Christ. He is our standard.

Every time the idea of holiness is presented in the Bible, standards are mentioned. We can't have a wonderful relationship with Christ without obeying him. When we were under the law and saw standards of holiness, we felt despair. The Spirit, however, gives us the power to attain these standards. Through the Spirit, we have life.

IS IT POSSIBLE FOR US TO BE HOLY?

Can anyone be holy? Yes! Every Christian is holy!

Can anyone be holy enough? No!

THE MEANING OF HOLINESS

To be "holy" means to be set apart for God. "Wholly" his. Sanctified. It is not so much of what we are set apart from, but what we are set apart to.

> *But you are a chosen generation, a royal priesthood,*
> *a holy nation. His own special people, that you may*
> *proclaim the praise of him who called you out of darkness*
> *into his marvelous light; who once were not a people,*
> *but are now the people of God, who had not obtained*
> *mercy, but now have obtained mercy.* —I PETER 2:9-10

MEASURING HOLINESS:

If our goal is to be more Christlike, can we move in that direction? Yes. If we're not holy enough now, can we be more holy this year than last? Yes. Our lives should show that we are moving in God's direction, showing more of God's presence in our lives.

We have to be a little careful, however, with visible indicators. We should serve God, have high morality, attend church, tithe, etc. but these don't prove holiness!

So what is the value of outward standards? They help reveal the absence of holiness! They can prove you are NOT holy, but won't prove that you ARE. They help indicate a Christian's maturity. They can show you are on the right course.

We had a young woman come into the church out of a life of wickedness and sin. She wore tons of makeup, short dresses, etc. But the people of the church just loved her, helped her and prayed for her. After a while, her skirts lengthened, her language changed, and the makeup wasn't quite so thick. She was being made into the image of Christ.

> *And I brethren, could not speak to you as spiritual people but as to carnal, as to babes in Christ. I fed you with milk and not with solid food; for until now you were not able to receive it, and even now you are still not able; for you are still carnal. For where there is envy, strife, and divisions among you, are you not carnal and behaving like mere men?* —I CORINTHIANS 3:1-3

God places high requirements for leadership. For God, the direction of our life is more important than the accomplishments of our life. Leadership is validated by character. Leaders gain influence from holiness. If you want God to use you and let your life be a mighty witness for him, you must attain standards of holiness.

HOW MUCH HOLINESS IS REQUIRED
FOR MINISTRY?

There are four common dangers:

1. Waiting until you are perfect to do anything for God.
    - The result? Paralyses. Nothing ever happens

2. Seeing holiness as an end to itself.
    - The result? Only internal growth, no fruit coming from your life

3. Expecting holiness to generate ministry.
    - The result? Dead end. This is saying, "If God wants me to serve Him He knows where I am."

4. Relating effectiveness in ministry to reliance on outward accomplishments like fasting, etc.
    - The result? Pride and self-centeredness.

There are five principles for ministry:

1. Be sure you have a proper relationship to God.
    - Not a perfect one, but a proper one

2. Confess all known sins.

- Let the Holy Spirit speak to you. Some people don't feel good, unless they feel bad! That's not God's way! Don't be conned into a state of condemnation all the time.

3. Seek healing for persistent sins.
    - If there's something you can't get free of on your own, put your pride away, confess your sins, get help and be free!

4. Allow others to read your spiritual barometer.
    - Don't be *too* open to the public, but do find a spiritual brother or sister that you can share with very honestly. Be willing to hear some criticism along with some praise.

5. The higher the leadership God will take you, the higher the standards become. There's an old song, "Deep and Wide." The wider your ministry becomes, the deeper your relationship should be to Christ.

CHRISTIAN PERFECTION

In dealing with sanctification (holiness) John Wesley used the term "Christian perfection." This scares some people! He didn't mean by this that we must be perfect in every area of our lives, but he meant that as we desire to please God and conform our lives to his will and to the image of his Son, we can reach a state where we love and serve God with all our heart, soul, mind and strength. It is a place where each decision of our lives is given to God, who is the center of our lives. We strive to bring our thoughts, words and actions under his control. Although we may not perfectly attain it, we must be reaching for it.

Along with personal holiness, John Wesley called for social holiness.

As Christians, faith is not to be quiet and private, but to cover the whole arena of our lives. We are to enter every area of human concern and bring the righteousness of God to bear upon that situation.

William H Willimon said it this way:

> In its very existence, the church serves the world, not by running errands, but by providing a light, that is, providing an imaginative alternative for society. The gospel call is an invitation to be part of a people who are struggling to create those structures which the world can never achieve through governmental power and balanced self-interest. By its very existence the church is a paradigm for a society, a demonstration which the world considers impossible.

We must perfect our lives in holiness. We live together in the church as a people who have already tasted the Kingdom. We demonstrate by who we are, what we say, and how we live that there is a Kingdom reality that transcends all earthly systems and programs. The church ought to present a picture to the world of what God wants the world to be. "Thy Kingdom come, Thy will be done, on earth as it is in heaven."

Where do we start? With ourselves!

QUESTIONS FOR REFLECTION:

1. Are you going on to perfection? Why or why not?

2. If Jesus were to come to your home today, what things might you want to change?

3. Is there any part of your life that is serving as a stumbling block or a barrier to others who may be ready to receive Christ?

4. Can others see Christian growth in you? Are you further along the path today than you were yesterday?

5. How long must you be a Christian before you are ready to serve Christ?

6. Are you experiencing Cognitive Dissonance? Strive to shorten the gap between what you know to be true and what you are actually doing and believing.

STEWARDSHIP AND TITHING

If you are a serious Christian, you should know what the Bible says about giving, and indeed, it has much to say to you:

> *But who am I and who are my people that we should be permitted to give anything to you? Everything we have has come from you, and we only give you what is yours already!* —I CHRONICLES 29:14

> *Honor the Lord with your substance, and with the first fruits of all your increase; so shall your barns be filled with plenty...* —PROVERBS 3: 9,10

> *One man gives freely, yet gains even more; another withholds unduly, but comes to poverty. A generous man will prosper; he who refreshes others will himself be refreshed.* —PROVERBS 11:24,25

For if you give, you will get! Your gift will return to you in full and overflowing measure, pressed down, shaken together to make room for more, and running over. Whatever measure you use to give–large or small–will be used to measure what is given back to you. —LUKE 6:38 (TLB)

But remember this–if you give a little, you will get a little...Everyone must make up his own mind as to how much he should give. Don't force anyone to give more than he really wants to, for cheerful givers are the ones God prizes. —2 CORINTHIANS 9:6,7

Remember the words of the Lord Jesus, that He Himself said, 'It is more blessed to give than to receive." —ACTS 20:35B

One little known reference to this principle of returning a portion of one's income to God is found in Genesis 14:18-20, which dates back long before the Jewish law dealing with giving. It sets the pattern for all giving in the bible.

Abram had just rescued his nephew, Lot, from the bloodthirsty King Chedorlaomer. Returning from his victory, Abram was greeted and blessed by still another king, King Melchizedek, who was a priest of the God of Highest Heaven. (Genesis 14:18)

Abram was so overwhelmed at Melchizedek's blessings that he immediately gave the king a tenth of his spoils, thus becoming the first example of tithing in God's word. A tenth is 10%.

The point you should note in this story is that God expressed his love for Abram through the generosity of Melchizedek. In the same manner, God expresses his generous spirit to you in countless ways. And so, in love and gratitude, you return—as Abram did—a portion of all God enables you to earn; you return it to him through your church for his work.

ALL BELONGS TO GOD

Too often we think that what we earn is ours to keep, forgetting that everything belongs to God and that we're only temporary stewards. Psalm 24:1 reminds us: "The earth belongs to the Lord and everything in it is his."

The principle is further emphasized in Leviticus, one of the most important as well as most difficult books in all the Bible. It presents God's plan for his chosen people: "A tenth of the produce of the land, whether grain or fruit, is the Lord's and is holy...And the Lord owns every tenth animal of your herds and flocks and other domestic animals." (Leviticus 27:30-32)

Translated today this means that whatever you earn, from salary or wages, or interest or dividends, etc—part of it belongs to God.

WE SHOULD TITHE BECAUSE:

The tithe is God's. If we don't tithe, we rob God. (Malachi 3:8-10)

God commands us to tithe. When we don't tithe we are being disobedient to God. If you try to obey God in other parts of your life but fail here, you are not faithful and spiritual growth is incomplete.

1. Tithing is an act of love. When we consider what great things God has done for us, out of love and gratitude we return our tithes and offerings to him.

2. Because tithing recognizes God's ownership of all of our lives. The tithe is described as the first fruits; meaning, a person gives to God the first of the harvest. We demonstrate this dedication as we tithe. We don't *give* our tithes, we pay them. Our offerings are beyond the required tithe.

3. Tithing is good business. We can never out give God. The more we give to Him, the more He gives back to us. When we tithe, we go into business with God. When we invest one tenth of our income, he promises to "open the windows of heaven and pour out a blessing." Malachi 3:10.

4. Just as the perils of money can cause frustration and worry, God's plan provides peace and freedom. This is not to say that a Christian's life will be financially trouble-free. We are human and subject to making mistakes. But once God is in charge of our finances, his divine correction and provision will bring this area under control.

There are steps you can take to put your finances under God's direction. First of all:

TRANSFER OWNERSHIP TO GOD

Christians must realize there is no substitute for this step. If you believe you are the owner of even a single possession, then the ups and downs affecting that possession will be reflected in your attitude. If, however, you have made a transfer of all ownership to God, you will realize that the event is God's way of moving providentially to accomplish his will in your life.

GET OUT OF DEBT

A scriptural condition of debt exists when any of the following circumstances are true:

- …money, goods, or services are owed to other people with payments past due.

- …The total of unsecured liabilities exceeds total assets (in other words, if a calamity took place, you would have a negative financial balance.

- …Financial responsibilities produce anxiety. God will give you a sense of peace when finances are managed according to His will.

EVALUATE EVERY PURCHASE BEFORE BUYING (Proverbs 18:15)

- Does it enhance God's work through you?

- Is it a necessity?

- Is it the best buy available?

- Does it add to your family relationships?

- Will it depreciate quickly?

- Will it require costly upkeep?

Use a written budget (Proverbs 16:9) How does this verse apply to maintaining a written budget?

Let God guide you in your purchases. Certainly you need clothing, food, transportation, insurance, some recreational things for you and your family and so on, but God can even give direction in the purchase of every day items.

Excel in your work. It is impossible to be slothful if excellence is the minimum acceptable standard. We should do everything as if the Lord himself were our employer. If he were (and he is!) what kind of work would we do? Would we get to work on time? How would we approach each task?

Use the abilities God has given you in the best possible ways to bring income into your home. Learn, study, try to excel and make the most of your talents. Then be quick to give God the glory for your success, and give him the first 10% of the increase your efforts bring.

Have a balanced commitment. Imbalance in life leads to frustration and problems. Family relationships should not be sacrificed in order to gain money. God wants US first, not our money. Families need PARENTS, not just providers. We have times to work, but we also need times to rest and interact with others. Seek the balance God requires.

Money can provide great freedom to meet the needs of our families and others, to extend the Kingdom of God and to make our lives more fulfilling. It can also bring great bondage, frustration and worry. God wants us to have wisdom in our financial dealings. We will have to battle our natural inclinations and pray that God will direct us if we are to have victory in this area.

Natural inclinations that lead to financial bondage	Principles of wisdom that lead to financial freedom
Deciding whether I can afford to tithe part of my money to the Lord	WISDOM is realizing that all my money belongs to God and that he will demonstrate his power through it only as I obey the principles of Scripture in managing it—including tithes and offerings
Borrowing money for depreciating items on the basis that I have the ability to pay it back out of future paychecks	WISDOM is avoiding any borrowing for depreciating items because this presumes upon the future and is warned against in Scripture since I don't know what each day will bring
Trusting God to supply money for debts I incurred through credit buying	WISDOM is selling or returning credit items and replacing them with ones I can afford—using the remaining debts as a classroom to force me to learn financial principles
Visualizing items I would like to buy if I ever have the money to afford them	WISDOM is learning to be content with food and clothing and purposing to use any additional funds according to God's clear direction
Loaning money to a friend if he has a worthwhile need for it	WISDOM is realizing that loaning to my friend would be putting him under bondage as my servant and thus getting clearance from the Lord to give him what I can as a gift instead
Investing an insignificant amount in chances and lotteries that go to worthwhile causes that might give me extra funds	WISDOM is discerning that everyone who attempts to make money through a program of chance is a loser. If I win, I establish a precedent for others and a philosophy for myself that God promises not to bless. If I don't win, I am being unfaithful in little amounts that God warns will result in mishandling large amounts

There are different kinds of giving in the Bible:

- Tithe—10% of all of our income

- Offerings—above the tithe that can be given to ministries, etc.

- Charity—God said whatever you give to those in need, he will give back to you

First Fruits: When you get a raise, or some unexpected increase, the first portion of that should be given to God as a one-time gift.

> *"Anyone who can be trusted in little matters can also be trusted in important matters. But anyone who is dishonest in little matters will be dishonest in important matters. If you cannot be trusted with This world's wealth, who will trust you with true wealth? And if you cannot be trusted with what belongs to someone else, Who will give you something that will be your own? You cannot be the slave of two masters... You cannot serve God and money."* —LUKE 16:10-13

JOHN WESLEY taught a great deal about money, just as Jesus did. The heart of his teaching comes down to a little saying:

GAIN all you can...
 SAVE all you can...
  GIVE all you can

GAIN ALL YOU CAN:

If God has given you talents and abilities to make money in honorable ways, then do it. Use those abilities to gain all that you can.

SAVE ALL YOU CAN:

Don't be wasteful. Get good value for all that you buy. Use everything to its best advantage. Know where your money is going. Save part of your earnings. (Remember that Jesus directed them to pick up the fragments when he multiplied the loaves and fishes so that nothing would be wasted.)

GIVE ALL YOU CAN:

John Wesley said that as Christians come to know the Lord and come under God's principles, they will increase their standard of living. (This is true: the Gospel lifts the standard of living of all people wherever the Gospel has been preached). He said that as people begin to give, God will always give more in return. This is the only way to safeguard people from getting caught up in money instead of being caught up in God. If people don't become givers, their increased finances would gain their heart and soon turn them aside from the Gospel. But if they remain faithful to giving all they can, they will stay true to the things of God.

APPLICATION:

1. What basic possessions would you need in order to experience content-
    ment? (I Timothy 6:8)

2. What experience have you had in seeing God provide specific financial
    needs in answer to your prayers?

3. Have you ever felt God directing you to give a specific amount to some
    person or work?

4. The Bible talks about bringing your money into the "storehouse." Today
    this is interpreted to mean the church. Do you believe your tithes and
    offerings should be given to the church? Why or why not?

5. Along with the church, *parachurch* organizations are providing much
    needed ministry in this world that the church isn't always able to provide.
    What should Christians do about funding these?

YOUR MINISTRY OF SERVICE

Fellow believer, you are something special. You are important to God and to the growth of His wonderful Kingdom. You have a unique partnership of ministry in building up the Body of Christ

Unfortunately, many Christians are unemployed in the kingdom of God. The purpose of this lesson is to help you discover that you have a place of ministry and to show how you can prepare yourself for that responsibility.

Contrary to common belief, Christianity is not a spectator sport. There are many, however, who attend church merely as pew sitters and sermon tasters. But the Scripture is clear in teaching that every believer is a minister and has a ministry. YOU ARE A MINISTER.

"The major challenge for Christians is not to do something
for the church, but to be the church." —F. C. MATHER

The laity are not IN the church.
   They are not FOR the church
      They don't do things AT the church.
      They ARE the church.

The church didn't invent ministry. It was modeled for her. As the founder and head of the church, Christ was always ministering: "I came to serve, not to be served." —Mark 10:45

All ministry must begin with the Body of Christ: By each other, for each other, to each other, and reaching beyond each other to those outside.

THE CHURCH IS MINISTRY:

1. Touching: Being willing to reach out to those needing help
2. Caring: being willing to be inconvenienced for others
3. Knowing: Being willing to be vulnerable and to be patient with those whose vulnerability calls for our ministry

Look up the six titles of a Christian found in I Peter 2:4,5,9, 10

1.

2.

3.

4.

5.

6.

WHAT IS YOUR CALL TO MINISTRY?

God has given us a variety of gifts so that we can respond to his call to ministry. We should remember that they are truly gifts. We do nothing to merit them. What we must do, however, is to discover them, develop them and be willing to use them for the benefit of others.

Look up spiritual gifts mentioned in Romans 12:6-8, Ephesians 4 and I Corinthians 12. As you read about these gifts, consider which gifts you may have.

How available are you for God to use? How sensitive are you to the needs and ministries of others? In what area can you most effectively serve the church?

THREE MINISTRY PRINCIPLES

1. Do everything to glorify God, not yourself
2. Make serving others the purpose of your work of service
3. Let Jesus touch others through you as you serve

MINISTRY IS NOT:	...MINISTRY IS:
Being recruited	Recognizing a call
Being coaxed	Discovering a gift
Being elected	Being equipped
Being used	Serving others
Being frustrated	Being fruitful

Pray and seek the guidance of the Holy Spirit as you seek to understand where God might want you to minister to meet the needs of others and to expand the Kingdom of God.

"Without God, we cannot; Without us, God will not." —St. Augustine

When we join the church, four things are asked of us: Our prayers, our presence, our gifts and our service. To be a fully-rounded, mature Christian, none of these should be left out.

GROWTH COMES THROUGH MINISTRY

One of the greatest joys of being a Christian is to watch God use us and produce spiritual fruit through us. Fil in the blanks and discover how you can be used by God:

1.   Matthew 22:37-39 tells us there are two choices we must make if we are to be effective in useful service:
2.   Romans 12:1-2 God calls each of us to two definite commitments: What are they?
3.   What is the prerequisite of having a great ministry for God? I Corinthians 13:

SHARING YOUR FAITH

The overflow of the spirit-filled life is sharing with others about this new life in Christ. Your devotional life, extended times of prayer, and prompt obedience to God will give your life an attractiveness which adds credibility to your words. Effective witnessing also involves skills. Skills can be learned and sharpened. You will become a sharpened instrument in God's hand as you receive training and gain experience in witnessing.

Acts 1:8 "The Holy Spirit will come upon you and give you power. Then you will be my witnesses in Jerusalem, in Judea, in Samaria, and the ends of the earth."

THE CHALLENGE:

A witness in a courtroom is expected to tell what he knows about a given situation. The Christian witness is to tell others what he knows about Jesus Christ and what it means to personally trust him.

1. What was the first thing Andrew did after he met Jesus? (John 1:40-42)
2. Why was Paul not ashamed to share Christ? (Romans 1:16)
3. What does a witness tell the people? (Acts 22:15).

WHY WITNESS?

1. **CHRIST TAUGHT IT**
   a) Christ's first instructions to his new followers: Mark 1:17
   b) Christ's last instructions to his new disciples: (Acts 1:8)

2. **THE WORLD NEEDS IT**
   a) What did our Lord command the church to do? (Matthew 28:20)
   b) What motivates believers to share their faith with others?
      (2 Corinthians 5:14)
   c) Why does the world need the gospel? (Matthew 9:12,13)

3. **CHRISTIANS DO IT**

   If a Christian is not a witness for Christ, he is disobedient to the will of God. Obedience is the fruit and proof of our love for Christ. A witnessing Christian is a happy, fulfilled Christian. Just as a little child is seen to be growing and maturing as speech begins to come, so Christians must learn to speak up for Christ or they will be immature and stagnant in their growth.

4. **GOD HONORS IT**

   Though you should always seek to bring those who are interested to a definite commitment to Christ, do not feel discouraged when some refuse to receive him as their Savior. That is God's responsibility. It is your responsibility to tell them the good news with love and genuine concern. Sharing Christ should be a way of life for every Christian. When you wake up each morning, thank the Lord that He is in you and ask him to use your lips to speak of his love and forgiveness to others.

5. HEAVEN CELEBRATES IT

What happens in Heaven when one sinner repents? (Luke 15:7)

SO, HOW SHOULD YOU WITNESS??

WITNESS BY A CHANGED LIFE-STYLE

"Show me your redeemed life, and I'll believe in your Redeemer" —VOLTAIRE

Since we are God's children living in a warped and wicked age, our friends, family, neighbors, coworkers, etc. must be able to see a difference in us if they are ever to know of their own need of God. When we look, act and talk just like the world, how can God's glory be seen?

Life-style evangelism is bringing people to Christ through the continual out-flowing of your faith in everyday life by the power of the Holy Spirit.

There are three important ingredients to consider when sharing Christ as a way of life:

a) Be available
b) Be spirit-filled
c) Be aggressive

Don't wait for people to come to you. Go to them. Set aside quality time to share Christ with others each week. Simply meet people by showing your friendliness. Reach out to those of the same sex, interests, etc. Someone said it this way: Make a friend, be a friend, bring a friend to Christ.

WITNESS BY PRESENTING CHRIST

When people comment on our friendliness, joy, good humor, etc. don't take the credit for yourself; give the glory to Christ and present him as wanting to be their Savior too.

WITNESS BY PLANNED OBJECTIVE

Witnessing is presenting a person, not a plan or program. The power is in the gospel. (Romans 1:16). Some Christians are constantly being used of God to introduce others to Jesus, because they have been trained to talk about Christ in the power of the Holy Spirit. They do not become distracted by discussing nonessential matters. There are many excellent tracts which present the gospel to the non-believer in a systematic way. Find a "plan of salvation" that is comfortable for you. Memorize the Scriptures involved, think of how you can tell your testimony in a brief manner and be prepared. God will use your readiness and willingness.

When you consider your testimony, think about the following:

1. What life was like before I met Jesus
2. Why and how I received him into my life
3. How my life is changed because of Jesus

Whenever you are alone with a person for a few minutes, you can assume that God has placed you there to reflect the good news of his love and forgiveness. Since Christ lives within us, we can simply ask him to give us the courage to speak for him.

Here is a simple way to present the gospel:

> *"The Bible says there are four things you and I must do*
> *to have new life, and know we are going to heaven."*

Step One; Repent. Acts 3:19 says, "Repent then and turn to God so that your sins will be wiped out.

- The first step in knowing where you are going is to make a U turn.

- Being sorry enough to confess you are a sinner and need God's forgiveness.

Step Two: Believe. John 3:16 "For God so loved the world that He gave his one and only son that whosoever believes in him should not perish but have eternal life."

- The reason we should believe in him is love. Jesus died in our place

- And that proves his love for us.

Step three: Confess. I John 1:9 "If we confess our sins, he is faithful and just to forgive our sins and to cleanse us from all unrighteousness."

- Our confession is not to man, but to God, for only God can forgive us.

Step four: Receive. John 1:12 "But as many as received him, to them he gave the power to become the sons of God."

- Nothing is ours unless we are willing to receive it.

APPLICATION:

1. Why do you think so few Christians lead others to Christ?

2. How does sin affect our witness for Christ?

3. What is the role of prayer in bringing others to Christ?

4. Apply Mark 1:17 (command) and Acts 1:8 (promise) to your life.

CONGRATULATIONS!

YOU HAVE DONE WELL! It wasn't an easy task going through each of these foundational lessons and answering the questions, etc. These topics however, are ones that you need to incorporate into your life if you are to remain a victorious Christian.

Never forget, however difficult it may seem at times, the great blessings and riches that are now yours as a Child of God. As God's child, these blessings include:

1. GUARANTEED SALVATION (John 10:28)
2. HE WILL SUPPLY EVERY NEED (Philippians 4:19)
3. THE PRIVILEGE OF PRAYER (James 5:16)
4. THE PROMSIE THAT CHRIST IS ALWAYS WITH US (Matthew 28:20)
5. STRENGTH FOR EVERY TASK (Colossians 1:11)
6. MEMBERSHIP IN THE KINGDOM OF HEAVEN (Colossians 1:13)
7. THE FORGIVENESS OF EVERY SIN (Colossians 1:14)
8. HAVING THE VERY MIND OF CHRIST (Philippians 2:5)
9. THE ABILITY TO INFLUENCE A NATION (Philippians 2:15)\
10. PREDESTINATED TO GLORY (Ephesians 5:5,6)

11. KNOWLEDGE OF THE WILL OF GOD (Ephesians 1:9)

12. AN INHERITANCE IN HEAVEN (Ephesians 1:11)

13. MORE GOOD THINGS THAT YOU HAVE EVER IMAGINED (Ephesians 3:20)